The 51 Shades of Love

A Collection of Poems

AF581480

Sanjana Prabhakar

INDIA • SINGAPORE • MALAYSIA

Copyright © Sanjana Prabhakar 2024
All Rights Reserved.

This book has been published with all efforts taken to make the material error-free after the consent of the author. However, the author and the publisher do not assume and hereby disclaim any liability to any party for any loss, damage, or disruption caused by errors or omissions, whether such errors or omissions result from negligence, accident, or any other cause.

While every effort has been made to avoid any mistake or omission, this publication is being sold on the condition and understanding that neither the author nor the publishers or printers would be liable in any manner to any person by reason of any mistake or omission in this publication or for any action taken or omitted to be taken or advice rendered or accepted on the basis of this work. For any defect in printing or binding the publishers will be liable only to replace the defective copy by another copy of this work then available.

Love is patient, love is kind
It makes you follow your heart and not your mind
Love is a blessing, sometimes a curse
Once you're broken hearted nothing feels worse

and i knew i was healing
when your words didn't have the same effect on me as they used to
when I could finally smile when i thought of her with you
when the tears were not blinding me like they did before
I knew I was healing when I did not need you anymore

i learnt this year
how fragile yet strong the human heart is
even after being broken several times
it dares to love again

sometimes i long to hold the little girl I was
who wanted nothing more than someone
to guide her through challenging times

i dread the day i will look at you
and feel nothing
it's also the day i look forward to the most

the pain too will wither away
so will all the love that once consumed me
and life will keep going like it always does

and you will never know how many times I broke myself just to build you up

how many times I picked you up while I was falling

how many times I swallowed my tears just to keep your tears from falling

how many times I came to hold you when no one else was calling

I knew something had changed

when I went from spending nights excited about seeing you the next morning

to wondering what you were doing all night

in the darkness of despair
in the most turbulent love affair
my mind will always think of us
of what could be but never was
of the remnants of my heart that remained
of the parts of my soul that you stained

it's as if my heart recognised yours
the moment we met
when our hands touched
it is a moment I can never forget

i hide all alone
it gets so hard to face the world
your presence makes it easier
its as if you weren't the reason
i went into hiding in the first place

i think of her in your arms
you whispering sweet nothings in her ear
like you did mine
i wonder then, if i ever cross your mind
when you look at her, do you see me sometimes?

words you said, words you didn't

words you wished to take back but words you couldn't

words that punched a hole through my heart remain etched in my mind

These wretched words, from which, not a single escape I can find free me now, let me go wont you?

why do you come back? when you promise not to

she has your heart so keep her close

forget the fact that I supported you through your highs and lows

stop trying to make peace after what you have done

this was a game for you.

Congratulations! you won.

you could have waited or walked away before you fell in love with another

you could have saved me from the agony of losing my lover

just given it a month or two, to fully recover

yet you just threw me six feet under

you know the truth, every last bit of it
you know who hurt who
but if you want me to take the blame
then for your happiness, I'll do the same

I told you my vulnerabilities
hid in a corner crying
when you used them as a weapon
to break me

on the hard days
I hold onto the fragmented pieces of your love
that still remain somewhere but are slowly fading from my memory

they said love was gentle and kind
you said you loved me
Either you were lying
or they were

and in this life, will i ever find what I truly need
or will I always stay right here, in this very place
asking the same question over and over and over again

And it feels as though
The day I found out the truth about her
Was the last time I was awake
Every moment has been a blur since
It's like living a nightmare that I can't seem to wake up from

I never want to see you again
I repeated, never in a million years
only to come back to you
in the same way
at the same place at the same time

you reappeared one day when I least expected it

the pain, the joy, the unwavering grief, every emotion known to mankind stirred up inside me

it confused me

now i know, what it is to love someone so much you turn your back on yourself just to be able to face them again

and if I were to choose between you and I
I would drown to keep you afloat
I would abandon myself to let you in once again
I would be to you what you could never be to me
A lover, a friend, a confidante and everything in between
I would choose you, only you, always you
even if you never chose me

you took my heart and made it yours
you didn't wait for reason or cause
I lost my breath as the waves of your love swept me off my feet
before I could come up for another breath
you were nowhere to be seen
I was left wondering what could have been

the pain comes in sudden gushes and radiates all throughout my body and then it leaves for awhile.

i start to feel okay until it returns in the same way and leaves me light headed.

when you looked me in the eye and uttered lies after lies,
did your heart ache a little?
when you made elaborate plans so that i wouldn't find out the reality of your deeds. did you ever hurt for me?

when i sleep, my soul is awake, my insides burn,
and i wake up with a jerk.
The tears flow.
i could fill oceans with these tears.

i didn't know a broken heart could physically hurt this much.
its as if the pieces of my heart were made of glass.
and now that they are shattered,
they pierce through every part of my body.

as I grow older, the more i learn
what I lost and all that I yearn
where was this wisdom all this while
why was I hiding my brokenness with a smile

and when i see you i might stumble, because i wouldnt recognize the person in front of me.

you would seem familiar but none I know.

you were a fantasy, i saw what you wanted me to see, but ever since reality has hit. I'm grieving. I'm grieving the fictious version of you that I made a life with.

that I wrote poetry for. that i made a home with in my mind.

I fell in line to make everyone happy
but when my turn came
they all broke the line
the more i tried to get ahead
the further I got left behind
that was, I learnt
the cost of putting everyone before yourself

and one day you'll look for true love
and you'll think of me
searching for the love I gave you
in every person you meet
but please don't try coming back
because I'd be long gone
because i'm finding myself now
I know what i deserve and how

i knew that was the last time
when I hugged you crying and you didn't even hug me back
you asked me to get it together and walked back inside
I wiped my tears and forced a smile on my face
I knew then I would never want to see you again

and that my dear was a devastating tragedy
when I loved you so completely
that I thought it was okay for you to not love me back
that my love would make up for all the love you lack

now the days are quieter and the rooms are empty
your smile is just a faint memory
tears are all that I associate with your essence
letting you go is a form of penance
for breaking my heart with my own bare hands
for allowing you to stay when I knew it was a mistake
now I sit here and seek forgiveness for being my own enemy
for searching for love where there was no empathy

it's a boon yet a curse to feel so deeply.
every waking moment is more agonizing than the next.
love seems like a fallacy.
none of it was, is or could be real.

intoxication doesn't help you forget
it doesnt erase the regret
it may distract you from your grief
it brings temporary relief
it is an illusion of healing
which is impossible without truly feeling
every memory that is hard to face
even broken hearts can heal with grace

Days on end i begged for you to be better
I wrote you letter after letter
showed you how much I was hurting
yet it didn't change a thing
and the last time you never came home when you said you would
I knew it was time to do what I always could
to let you go to her, the one you wanted instead
you pursued her all this time while knowing I cried every night in my bed
you say its my fault but you never let me in
always finding faults within me, with you I could never win
you thought you were superior and I wasn't good enough
I saw it in your eyes, I saw it in your love

while the trees shed their leaves and the seasons change
every season brings with it something strange
something to remember, something to forget
some happy times, some regrets

making the same decisions over and over again
I wonder what really was I trying to attain
texts, calls, voice messages that I continued to send
nothing changed what happened in the end.

was it love was it passion
was it worth it, all this emotion?
was it an old pattern, or something true
since you left, I question everything, do you?

that night changed something in me
when you left me outside crying alone in the cold
I think I didn't want to believe that you didn't love me
even though it was clear as day
Now, no matter what you say
you will never again see me that way

sometimes i forget who I am
while trying to be who I am expected to be
maybe I've lost my individuality
maybe this is my new reality

After everything you have done
All that comes to mind is
I promised you my heart
I suppose I was never good at breaking promises after all

When you sit and cry silently
Breaking down in your mind violently
Fighting battles that you wanted to win

Reliving it all every day
Like it would never leave, like it was here to stay

So you choke up everytime you speak
Smiling even with tears rolling down your cheeks
You never let them know and they think all is fine
While you tell yourself, these silent battles are only mine

But then it starts to get better, and you do it on your own
And that's the beauty of it, and how much you've grown

You are home to me
Waited for you for what seemed like a century

You're everything and more
Every laugh, every tear, everything I adore

I can live without you
But I don't want that
Cause my heart is always going to be wherever you are at

No day can ever go by when I don't stop and think about you
You have become the reason for my existence too

All the promises you made but didn't keep
What you sow is what you shall reap
Enough of sorrow enough of this grief
Love will blossom when I arrive
I'm done sitting on the sidelines, now is my time to thrive

I come alive when you're next to me
This feeling is something I can't believe
When i look into your eyes
Every fear suddenly dies

Holding you close to me is my happy place
A beautiful home, a safe space
I waited for a long time for you
To be immersed completely in you is the least I could do

I never want to let you go
I may try to not let it show
But it's magic everyday
Being yours in every fucking way

To forever and beyond.

sometimes i wonder if i have ever known
what love truly is
or was I just romanticizing something ordinary to feel what I always longed to feel

When the truth is more painful than the lies
Something inside you dies
Your whole body becomes numb
It is an out of body experience for some

But acceptance follows shortly
And the truth starts settling in
Life starts anew and love will blossom again

To all the hopeless romantics, Never give up on love.

www.ingramcontent.com/pod-product-compliance
Lightning Source LLC
LaVergne TN
LVHW041253150826
845673LV00008B/2565

* 9 7 9 8 8 9 3 2 2 2 0 7 4 *